IMAGES

Materials

Karen Bryant-Mole

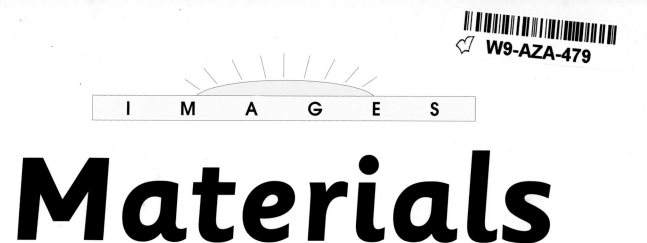

Silver Press
Parsippany, New Jersey

First published in Great Britain by Heinemann Library, an imprint of
Heinemann Publishers (Oxford) Ltd., Halley Court, Jordan Hill, Oxford OX2 8EJ, U.K.

© BryantMole Books 1996
Designed by Jean Wheeler
Commissioned photography by Zul Mukhida
Printed in Hong Kong
00 99 98 97 96
10 9 8 7 6 5 4 3 2 1

Published in the United States in 1997 by Silver Press
A Division of Simon & Schuster
299 Jefferson Road
Parsippany, NJ 07054

Library of Congress Cataloging-in-Publication Data

Bryant-Mole, Karen.
   Materials/by Karen Bryant-Mole.
      p.   cm. — (Images)
   Includes index.
   Summary: Photographs as well as simple text introduce a variety of materials such as
wool, glass, and paper.
   ISBN 0-382-39587-5 (LSB)—ISBN 0-382-39623-5 (PBK)
      Materials—Juvenile literature. [1. Materials.] I. Title. II. Series: Bryant-Mole, Karen.
   TA403.2.B78   1997   95-51186
   620.1—dc20   CIP
                                                                                 AC

Some of the more difficult words in this book are explained in the glossary.

Acknowledgments
The Publishers would like to thank the following for permission to reproduce photographs. Chapel Studios,
5 (right), 10 (right), 17 (left); Positive Images, 10 (left), 11 (left); Tony Stone Images, 4 (left); Larry Ulrich,
5 (left); Bob Thomas, 11 (right); Roslav Szaybo, 16 (left); Nicholas DeVore, 16 (right); Jean-Marc Truchet,
17 (right); Peter Correz, Zefa, 4 (right).

Every effort had been made to contact copyright holders of any material reproduced in this book. Any omissions
will be rectified in subsequent printings if notice is given to the Publisher.

Contents

Liquids

Liquids are usually wet.

Water is a liquid.

Paint and
bubble mixture
are liquids, too.

5

Solids

Solids can't be poured. They have a shape that usually stays the same.

Look around you. Can
you see some more solids?

Plastic

Plastic is waterproof.

It is strong
and light.

Plastic can be
made into all
sorts of shapes.

Wood

Wood comes from trees.

It is often used to make buildings and furniture.

Wool

Wool comes from sheep.

It has to be spun
and then dyed.

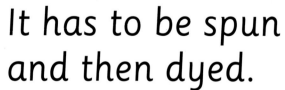

It can be
used to make things
like this wooly hat.

Metal

There are many different types of metal.

stainless steel

silver

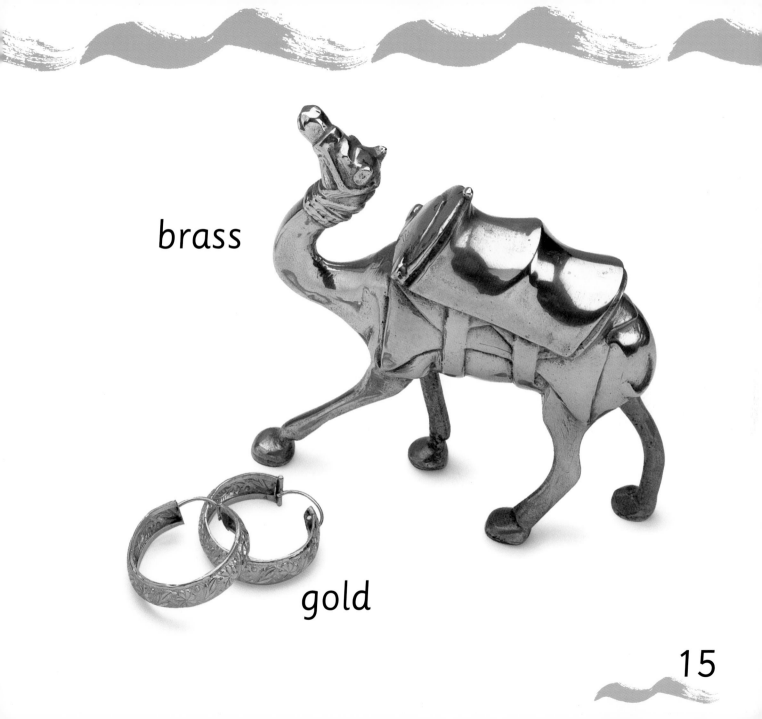

brass

gold

15

Fabric

Some fabrics, like cotton and silk, are made from natural materials.

Other fabrics, like polyester and nylon, are synthetic.

Glass

Glass can be colored or clear.

You can usually see
through clear glass.

Paper

some books   some tissues

a birthday card

a paper plate

All of these things have been made from paper.

Clay

Clay can be worked into lots of different shapes.

Glossary

dyed made into a particular color
material what an object is made from
spun pulled out and twisted
synthetic not a natural material
waterproof won't let water through

Index